THE MAKING OF A

CARIBBEANPRENEUR

Strategies for Overcoming Fear

and Building Wealth

Nerissa Golden

All photos by © Bevil Byam, St. Maarten, Netherlands Antilles

Cover Art by BlueOrange Design, St. Maarten, Netherlands Antilles

The Making of a Caribbeanpreneur: *Strategies for Overcoming Fear and Building Wealth*

ISBN: 1453769501

A TrulyCaribbean.Net Production

Dedication

To the Caribbeanpreneurs that rock! Carol Mitchell on computer keys (programmer turned children's author); Loic Bryan on easel with colored pencils, acrylics, and graphics; Kaishah Peters on the runway with her crocheted designs; Gregory Richardson also on computer keyboard and always armed with a cheaper and more secure way of doing things; Reuben Rogers on bass; and Susan Barnes-Pereira bringing the moves no matter the obstacles she faces.

Acknowledgements

Thank you Dad for teaching me a whole lot about money, many times without saying a word.

Lord, you are the Master Entrepreneur who gives me witty inventions and sees way beyond my fears to my successes.

Holy Spirit, you are wisdom and the best teacher.

Jesus, the best Big Brother who showed me I could overcome fear because you did it first.

Contents

The Making of a
Caribbeanpreneur

The Monday after my first Young Entrepreneurs Symposium (YES 2006) found me scrounging around to find money to buy a pack of baby pampers. How could that be when I had just spent an amazing weekend encouraging other entrepreneurs to pursue their passions to make successful enterprises? YES 2006 had received record coverage locally, regionally and internationally and all that attended left energized and prepared to follow their dreams. Some realized going off to college would be the best investment they could make, while others turned their part-time ventures into full-time money-making enterprises. But I had nothing but press clippings and debt to show for my efforts.

When the idea first came to create YES, it was to encourage entrepreneurship in the Caribbean but also as an outlet for my passion to motivate others and sell my books. How could I sell a book if I had never written a book? I let the idea of the conference become bigger than my dream to write and so when everyone went home feeling great and motivated, I went home depressed, drained and definitely broke. Simply put, I had put the cart before the horse.

Gregory Richardson of St. Maarten, the Techpreneur who had won Most Outstanding Speaker at both YES 2006 and YES 2007 always recounts the years of his 'spectacular failures.' In his quest to make a business from his passion for computers and technology, he failed several times before his company Secure Tech International took off. Many of us don't want to remember those years but trust me they are vital to your future success. I have had some spectacular failures too in my business past. Some made the press and some didn't but they all taught me lessons that are priceless today.

The bible says that God will restore the years that the locusts have eaten and I used to think it meant that if I lost 10 years then God could make it all come back in one. It does mean that to a certain degree, but more so, the years you feel have been a total waste and full of failures, have actually been the training ground for the successes that are ahead for you.

You must consciously and systematically decide you are going to make money. It will not fall into your lap, it will not come from a pie in the sky but it will come if you make up your mind that with effort and perseverance you are going to be an entrepreneur.

One of the best gifts you can give yourself is freedom. True success is having the freedom to make good choices and carve out a future of your own making and to better others. I enjoy being able to work the hours I want then spend time with my children. It is a gift that I treasure to watch them grow up. One of the most unexpected ventures I have been involved with came from a desire to be with my children and play a larger role in their education. Victory Christian Academy is thriving today because I saw potential in a need that was shared by many other parents.

No matter how old or how young you are it is the right time to start a business. It does not have to become a full-time gig, it can be something that supplements your regular income and gives you more money for rainy days and an uncertain future.

This book contains a few of the lessons I have learned and continue to learn about making money, managing it and growing it. They did not come simply by reading the bible or other people's ideas on making money. In hindsight, I should have read more. But the truth is, like many young people today I require hands on experience and visual stimulation to get it. These lessons were learned in the school of real life; all with the purpose to change my life, my children's and this wonderful planet we call home.

God has a plan to prosper you and He set out in His Word strategies that can enable you to get there and stay there consistently and for a lifetime. It is my hope that the ideas and experiences I share will open the eyes of your understanding and you can see God's love and the wisdom of the Master Entrepreneur. I pray you will be encouraged to chart your own entrepreneurial course and enable you to turn your passions into a most rewarding enterprise.

What Daddy Taught Me
About Money and What Wealth Is

The Legacy

Have you heard the saying, "Do as I say and not as I do?" As a parent, I have found that this never works because inevitably my children will follow my habits; even the ones I am unaware of. It is often through watching and listening to them play and interact with each other that I become aware of bad habits or negative phrases that I use and need to change.

One of the most important men in my life has been my father. He is a complex (read: hardheaded, stubborn, tenacious, I'll stop there) individual and only a willingness to learn and query what makes him tick will result in the answers. If you take him only at face value, you will miss the lessons that are being taught. If you shy away from the tone and the words, you miss an opportunity to hone your skills on the rock that he is built from. He is in no way perfect. In fact the more I learn, the more I discover how human he is and that makes me love him more.

My father has baffled me with his ability to make the impossible very possible and in the most practical of ways. Many of the examples in this book, I learned from his sermons because we never sat down at home and discussed money. I also looked at the things he did to accomplish his goals to develop my own wealth building strategy. In some cases it was necessary to follow his methods but at other times I had to do the opposite. I have always wanted to know how he got to the place when even if his pocket was empty, he still had an attitude of abundance and no matter the challenge he always managed to triumph.

Paul says I have learned that whatever state I am in to be content (Philippians 4:11). He is not talking about being satisfied. Content is a poor translation as the original word used is derived from the word prosperous. Paul in essence said *I don't care how things look right now or the odds stacked against me, I have learned how to make my way prosperous and be self-sufficient.* You too can do this regardless of the economy and all of the bad news that seems to be so evident and despite your empty pocketbook.

Looking back in my own life I see the same pattern of abundance but I did not understand where it came from or how to harness and then preserve it. Instead my life was filled with too many moments of total lack and too few moments of provision. I have come to see that making money is not a lucky draw and you must have a strategy in place to create it and then maintain it.

Upon reflection, I remember when I graduated from high school at 15 and began to work my dad would encourage me to save my money and of course give something to the family. I was not having any of that. In retrospect, it would have been better for him to say every payday bring me fifty dollars to go on your savings and twenty to your mom. My unwillingness to save then meant that later when I began earning more money the discipline of putting away cash was not there. Today, I'd have a purse full of cash and a week later most if not all was gone and I was living at home with no expenses.

Many entrepreneurs believe that because they just got $500 in their hand for a job, they can run right out and get that new outfit or blow it on other stuff. That money is not yours to spend; it must go back into the business. You will need new equipment soon, pay the rent or invest in promotions. It makes no sense to always be back at square one at the start of each month.

If you can begin today to put cash away; no matter how little, it will be a lesson well learnt when your business begins to grow. It is also very important to teach your children how to save money. It is a discipline that is needed to employ the strategies given in this book. Discipline is created from making a decision to do the same thing each day, regardless of how you feel physically or emotionally. Eventually it will become a habit and will no longer take great effort for you to set aside money and reinvest in your business.

I will never forget Daddy's story about his dream to open a gas station in his village in Montserrat. In the early 90's, he was just completing work on his first house there, a project that took many years and was a miracle in itself, considering what he was making as a preacher. But when he felt God impressing him to build a gas station he quickly dismissed it as impossible and not even necessary as his village was remote and the island had other stations spread around the capital of Plymouth. The village of St. Johns was considered country. You were as likely to see donkeys and cars using the same roads in the same measure. My dad considered his lack of education, none existent finances and not a clue about where and how to start building a gas station and dropped the dream.

Fast forward five years to July 18, 1995, his beloved Montserrat is sent into a tailspin as Soufriere Hills volcano erupts. The capital and the surrounding villages in the East and South of the island are evacuated. Within two years more than two-thirds of the island is uninhabitable and life continues in the West and North. More than 8,000 people are forced to relocate to the United Kingdom, neighboring Antigua and other Caribbean islands, Canada and the United States.

My dad's small village becomes the center of operation on Montserrat. My old primary school is now the hospital, where I gave birth to my son in 2003. All major government offices, utility companies, banks are now within a stones throw of where his navel string and mine are buried and up until 2004, the only operating gas station on the island was now located in our tiny remote 'country' village of St. Johns. But it was not owned by my father.

I keep that story in my head when I want to talk myself out of following the dreams I am seeing. When I want to ignore that voice that says go ahead, you can do it. When I want to rationalize my way out and declare it cannot possibly work out the way I am seeing it. God wants to give us dreams bigger than ourselves, bigger than what we can accomplish on our own. He has a plan to bless you, so that others can be blessed but when all you consider is yourself and your abilities, you will miss what is waiting for you on the other side of a completed dream.

Many of you have your own "impossible " dream but it will remain so if you do not acknowledge that already placed within you is the power to do the impossible when you believe in yourself and the God who created you. Although you may be living in obscurity and the challenge of keeping food on the table takes super human effort please do not give up on your "impossible" dream. It isn't really. God can and will do exceedingly, abundantly above all you can ask or dream according to how you allow the power of His Son Jesus Christ to be manifested through you (Ephesians 3:20).

Lesson 1: Build a New Legacy

If we are to be truthful we must admit that our islands were built with the enduring spirit and energy that is the essence of Caribbean people. Our histories are all entwined as our brothers and sisters moved about from sugarcane plantations, to oilfields, hotels, and other industries to make a living.

What we also spread was a belief that we could never be more than what we could labor with our hands to provide and that someone from the outside would always have more than us. If we look around, we can see that many of our industries, most of our prime residential areas belong to foreigners. Many of our beaches are being cut off from public use. And as my Dad says, we have given up our coastlines. Wars are lost when you lose the control of your coasts. We are slowly being pushed inland as homes on the beaches are sold for millions and the rest goes to international corporations with the right connections and enough cash to change laws and buy politicians.

We need to confess that the choices our parents and further back to our forefathers made perpetuated a legacy of lack and a dependence on others to protect and provide for us. The Caribbean islands all began as colonies of European powers and it was most common to see whites holding all of the top positions. They were the educators, government leaders and ran the businesses we purchased from. It has been ingrained in our psyche that white is right. Even though many islands are now independent and it is common to see black teachers, lawyers, government leaders we still give deference to outsiders with the right accent and skin tone perceiving them to be more capable than our own people. I have had government officials say to me that they do not trust or will support the ideas from locals and even after being scammed time and time again by foreigners they deny their own the opportunity to make valuable contributions to their nation. It is time to build a new legacy.

God told Joshua, "Moses my servant is dead," (Joshua 1:2). Moses represented a stage of deliverance and also a place of provision that only came from the hands of God. If God did not send manna and quail, there was no food for the Israelites during their 40 years in the wilderness. If miracles did not occur, the waters were undrinkable. But eventually Moses died and it also ended an era of dependency and meant that the Israelites would now have to play a role in determining their destiny and providing for their own daily needs.

If we are to be totally spiritual, then in truth we are to always depend on God but because He gave us a body, we are more than spirit and so in the physical we must walk out this destiny. We cannot sit and say "God will make a way," we must now take the steps to see the total manifestation of His plan for us.

To do this, we must accept that the legacy of lack and dependency we were handed down will not do for us or the future survival of our children and our nations. We will forever be grateful for what was done but now we must be ready to take it further. We must reject those ideologies that have kept us enslaved long since emancipation day. We no longer work on plantations, but our sons and daughters are enslaved in the tourism industry in the lowest paid and ranked positions, while management and ownership posts are held by foreigners. Our children understand there must be more to life than slaving away for foreign land owners and big corporations, but they have interpreted this to mean that fast cash at any cost is a better option. So they have become enslaved to drugs, guns, prostitution and any type of living that ensures minimal work and the greatest financial gain. But they miss the fine print as they end up in physical and mental prisons both in the Caribbean and abroad for their illegal acts.

Those who do try to stay on the straight and narrow are met with the obstacles of small island mentality or the crabs in a barrel theory…quickly succumbing to the talk or turning around at the first road block created to stop the dream. With a ready arsenal of great excuses, we can explain away why we quit before getting out of the starting blocks, and everyone around us will accept it because it is what we have always done.

Decide today that you will get rid of your excuses and investigate every road block before deciding it is a dead end. The time it takes you to come up with an excuse to quit is the same amount of time you need to come up with a reason to press ahead.

Joshua was repeatedly told not to be afraid. I suffer with that same issue. I get afraid often. I am afraid most times I attempt something new…but God's promise to me is that "He will not fail me," (Joshua 1:5). That gives me confidence because I realize He has more invested in the outcome than I do. The story already ends that God wins and the Devil looses. His only desire is that we be a part of living the story and maintaining the victory. Make the commitment today, to move past your fears and live out your story.

Joshua needed to embrace the fact that Moses, the one that taught him everything he knew about leadership was gone. Just like the Israelites who were all born in the wilderness, his only dependency could be on God and he had to trust the instructions that he was given.

When I first began to study Joshua, it was 1997 and I had been impressed to leave my job as journalist for The Chronicle newspaper on St.

Maarten and start my own business. Talk about fear. I had just bought my first car, a shiny black Mitsubishi Colt with a brand new bank loan. I had also recently moved into my first apartment, so a lack of job security caused me no end of worry. But try as I might, I could not get away from that voice that said I needed to leave that job. In January of 1998, I turned in my resignation and February first found me in that apartment on my knees seeking God's direction as I had no idea where to begin. Of course with hindsight I can think of a thousand things I should have done to prepare for that time, but I was given no safety nets and I realize now that was the point, I was to look only to Him for direction.

I did not even own a computer, but I wanted to publish a magazine, I wanted to handle public relations and I had only one client, a consulting firm I had been freelancing with for the previous six months.

An amazing thing happened. As I got up each day and focused on the vision of owning my business and finding clients, my confidence grew and so did the work. That first month was hard. I spent most of my days on my knees and at night with their permission, I used The Chronicle's computers to work on my newsletters and other projects. If I told you at the end of every month I could pay my car note and rent on time, I would be lying. My phone was cut because I could not afford to pay the bill and in a moment of panic, I signed a contract with a company because no other work was coming my way. It was the most stressful three months of my life and the security I thought would come with it did not. Every month I still had to wait to get paid and some times the checks bounced on the first and second go round.

So you know who had to repent and tell God sorry for panicking and not waiting on Him. In the times when there was no work, I prayed and studied the Word. I had more time to visit with friends and I found I enjoyed having the freedom to go anywhere at anytime without having to be concerned about a boss. I watched God do many miracles during that time, I was able to travel to other places without ever spending a dime of my own money, and His provision for me was constant, even when the clients were not.

Lesson 2: Shut Down the Voices

People are not going to understand you. They will tell you that you are crazy, fanatical, and certainly not practical or realistic. I am all for practicality, but the first thing you will learn about God, is that to reach the places that you need to fulfill the story, you will have to go beyond what seems logical to you and others and just move.

He will always ask you to get to the end of yourself before He steps in and works. You get to decide if it happens at the last minute, or if upfront you just put every effort forward without hesitation and then wait for God to make the next move.

For the most part it won't be the average person on the street that will affect you. It will be those who are closest to you; your family members, significant other, friends, anyone that you look to for emotional and physical support will be the vessels used to shake you and sift you. It is not that they don't love you. What you are doing makes them afraid. You are challenging every notion that they grew up with about themselves and their place in the world. Your desire to follow nothing more than a dream is risky and they are fearful of your failure but also of your success. You dare to do what they used to dream of doing but no longer even bother to.

My magazine only lasted five issues. One too many negative comments from the people closest to me made me think I was doing something wrong. This despite the fact that women and men kept asking for me to continue the project and I had begun to gain advertisers and increased readership. You cannot allow other people's voices to be louder than your own or the voice of the Spirit of God within you.

If you are a Christian, the added judgments that come with pursuing dreams in non-traditional "Christian" permitted vocations will be many. How do you perform at a secular function, when Christians don't go to places like that? How do you explain that you want to get beyond only having enough to get by and to be able to change your community with much more than prayer? How do you convince people that there will be a demand for video games with total Caribbean vibes, language and locations in the near future? "You can't possibly earn a living from dancing or writing. Why don't you get a real job?"

The answer is that you don't have to prove anything to anyone but yourself. No answer you give will ever be enough to satisfy them. Only the reality of your success will tell the tale that you were not that crazy and you really can earn a living from dancing and writing and making video games. You cannot depend on others to support or encourage you. In fact, God will send the people who will support you in His time and usually it will be those who are outside your usual circle. He will separate you from those you are emotionally dependent on, because you need to learn how to trust yourself and Him. When you do, you will gain much more even among your family and peers. The temporary loss of that circle is worth the long term gain of prosperity in all areas of your life.

He promises to give us back everything we let go for the sake of the gospel (Mark 10: 28-30). The gospel simply put is that we are designed to live a life of victory in all areas. Jesus died and rose again, so we could worship God by fulfilling His plan through our lives, daily and victoriously.

Lesson 3: Pay Your Debts

Many parents are guilty of not teaching their kids about money. Our children usually know when there is no money but they don't understand that there is more to getting it than to pop an ATM card in a bank machine. The purpose of money and how to attain it must become part of our regular conversations with our children as well as family and friends. We need to be open about sharing lessons we have learned from mistakes so others don't have to repeat them.

Right up front I want to tackle the issue of debt. As much as possible, do not create any new debt. If you cannot afford it, do not buy it. If there is no cash in your hand to purchase it please do without it. This book will offer some ideas of how to start with minimal start-up and hopefully without having to go to the bank for a loan. You do not want to start out in debt as this creates undue stress and loss of energy that should be spent on building your business.

Even if the debts you now have are years old, it is important that you pay your debts. This speaks to your integrity and will be a discipline vital for the long term image and success of your business. This is the key to building not just your credibility but also the right attitude for dealing with money.

In the Caribbean, we tend to avoid creditors. We refuse to answer the phones and ignore late notice letters acting as if we do not acknowledge them, they will disappear. While living in England I learned that it is better to speak to your creditors, be it the phone company or your landlord. Let them know what is happening. If you can't pay the outstanding amount, commit to paying even a token fee so that they can see you are not planning to renege on your commitment and maintain your integrity until you can do better and pay the entire amount off. You will also find that every payment gets you closer to a resolution, and if you can, commit to changing your lifestyle to lower those bills where possible. I have also found that when I commit to a payment plan that is within my means, eventually a door opens which allows me to clear up the outstanding amounts in a much shorter space of time than expected.

Giving to others is also a proven method of receiving debt cancellation and supernatural provision. Read the story of the widow and the Prophet Elijah in 1 Kings 17: 11 – 16. Sounds strange, doesn't it, but God says that when we give to others He is obligated to return to us in the same measure. We will speak about giving in a later section.

Lesson 4: Know Your Worth

Where in St. Kitts Can You Find Someone Who Will Pay You 48,000 a Year? That question was asked to me in 2001, when I told a group of men who asked me to help them set up and run a non-profit foundation that I wanted to be paid EC$4000 a month. They said it was unheard of, especially for a woman to be paid that much. The worst of it was I could not justify it to myself why I should be paid that. I knew it was an amount that would allow me to take care of my young family and help as I started my public relations firm, but I did not believe I deserved it and I did not bother to challenge their opinion.

That question resounded in my ears for a long time because I wanted to be able to answer it and I did not know how. We are all much more than the balance on our bank statement and the cash in our purses. True wealth is internal but how do you quantify that in a world where everything is about the Benjamin's?

God's currency is not the worlds. The world says money and all of its trappings. God says love above all else. That same bible says "money answers all things" (Ecclesiastes 10:19) and later on the love of money is the root of all evil (1 Timothy 6:10). So which comes first or can it be both?

I have come to realize that when I see myself as infinitely valuable regardless of my bank account, my lack of a car, home, fine clothing, then I am wealthy. My greatest asset is me. The fact that I was created in the image of God makes me priceless. This is even before you add my winning personality, my smile, my passion for helping others, being a great mother and friend, and the list goes on. God said after He completed making the first man "it was very good" (Genesis 1:31).

Be accepting of this gift today, you were made "very good". Beyond just the physical design, God believed and still does that you are His image and so your very nature is that of creativity, passion and love. You are a problem solver, an over comer, a healer, you are the physical manifestation of Him. You will never have true wealth without this. Everything else can disappear but when your concept of wealth is built on who you are and who loves you most, which is your Heavenly Father then you can never be poor.

You must know your personal worth as well as your financial worth. That period of time in St. Kitts taught me first, that my work was and always deserves adequate compensation, and to undersell myself out of fear of not getting the job costs me more in the long run.

Anneke deBruin is a very enterprising woman who suggested to me that I sit down and list the things that I wanted to accomplish each month. Not just the bills and savings but how I wanted to spend my leisure time. When a value was given to each item then I had an idea of what my monthly income needed to be to allow for the life I desired. This was not easy for me to develop and it was quite a few years before I could adequately come up with a price scheme that fit my goals.

When you know what you are worth then you can ask confidently and expect to get what you want. Yes, I have turned down jobs because they didn't value my time or think my fees appropriate and I have also taken jobs for free or at a lower rate because I knew the long term benefit to me would be worth it. Never allow fear to be the reason you take or don't take a job. We will tackle and conquer this monster in the coming chapters, so keep reading.

Lesson 5: Opportunities are Every Where

Just as my concerns for my children's education led me to start Victory Christian Academy (www.academy.trulycaribbean.net) in 2006, your concerns can be the foundation on which you build your business dream. VCA was not about making profit and it still is not. That is why once I got it up and running I let it go and turned it over to the church where it is located on St. Maarten.

Your passions may not be about making money and that is quite alright. You probably have the makings of a social entrepreneur. What solutions can you bring to the ever increasing problem of teenage pregnancy, drug abuse, gang violence, latchkey children? Maybe you are concerned with the number of older people who live alone and seem to be abandoned by their children. Does the destruction of the environment just get you all motivated to start a recycling or anti-plastics drive? Then you can still find great reward by launching a non-profit organization in your community.

Just like a regular business, you need to have a strategy, the finances and the motivation to pursue it as it grows. There are opportunities all around you. The goal is to find the ones that spark your entrepreneurial engine.

Barrington Bennett (www.bennettltd.net) in the Cayman Islands is a contractor by trade but when his teacher wife told him of the number of children in the school system in need of speech therapy with the only recourse being to seek treatment in the United States, he saw an opportunity for a new venture. He invested the resources to hire a trained speech therapist and now offers a valuable service to families on his island through New Horizons.

Anderson Quarless wanted to tell stories through film. But with limited resources on his beloved Grenada he used his abilities as a videographer to make the island's first feature film "Blinded" about the tragedy and pain of domestic violence. Using his skills with a camera is opening doors for him around the region and helps to fund his passion for making movies.

Kaishah Peters (www.kaidesignsxm.com) from St. Maarten has a fashion degree but had to find work with the government to make a living. It was her grandmother that taught her to knit and now it has given her a niche in the growing market of Caribbean fashion designers. Her daytime job keeps her in crochet needles and thread so she can build Knitty Kitty. It is not enough for her to dress the daring women of St. Maarten. Through her website and with a consistent effort to attend at least three or four Fashion Weeks annually, her products and her brand has gone global. Already expanding, she creates her own soaps and lotions to make sure the women who wear her clothes not only look great but smell great too.

As a boy, Reuben Rogers (www.reubenrogers.com) could be found with all the other young musicians vying for playing time during the annual church conventions on St. Thomas. Luckily his mother also the bishop's wife never restricted his love for playing the bass to church events. Under the mentorship of other talented local musicians, Reuben played jazz at local hotels during the tourism season until he went off to pursue a degree at Berklee College of Music. Now this musical maestro is traveling the world with jazz greats such as Grammy Award winners Diane Reeves, Joshua Redman, Aaron Goldberg and Peter Martin.

There have been numerous road blocks and challenges to make Susan Barnes-Pereira give up her dream of running a successful dance studio. With perseverance and an unwavering good attitude and belief in her dream and a big God she has overcome them one move at a time. Even the challenges to her health created a new opportunity for business expansion. Now her Barnes Dance Academy on Grand Cayman offers much more than dance, she provides a holistic approach to living which touches body, mind, and spirit.

It may be a personal crisis that births your business dream, the needs of your children, a family member or a community. Ideas are all around you so be open to see them and also think outside the box. You are also not limited to the things that you have a degree in. Why not start the business and hire the right professionals for it to succeed? Your options are limitless.

Lesson 6: Sell Sell Sell

I hate selling or at least that is what I fooled myself into believing for a very long time. In college quite a few of my friends were taking marketing classes and I thought ughhh, I can't sell. Now that is all I do. I have to sell you the vision for you to even pick up this book and read it. I had to sell the concept of YES 2006, YES 2007, and Victory Christian Academy to get others to sign up. On more than one occasion it is what kept my family fed when there were no professional positions available.

While living in St. Eustatius in 2002, I was unemployed and money was low. It was a challenge to keep motivated when my dreams seemed as limited as the size of the island. There I was, driving a gorgeous gold Mercedes Benz and not being able to keep the lights on. I took the few dollars we had, purchased bread, cold cuts, cheeses, and sandwich bags and began selling the best sandwiches I have ever made to the medical students at the local university two streets from where we lived. At first it was only tuna and cheese I could afford. But after doing so well the first week, I was soon offering turkey and ham and a variety of chips and drinks. I will confess that having a cute baby on my arm was a good draw but they kept coming back because I had found a niche unfulfilled. The students had the money but no time to run down town to a restaurant for lunch. Look around to find the opportunities that you can fill.

Don't be afraid to sell yourself and your products. Believe in what you have and trust your ability to transfer that to others. Practice in the mirror, on your friends until your confidence grows. But it gets easier after the first try.

Lesson 7: It's All Been Done Before

There is nothing new under the sun. As much as we are advancing in technology the basic needs of man remain the same. You may have a new method of providing a service or product but there will always be the necessity to plan how you will increase your income, keep costs low and maintain the quality as your business grows.

I can remember starting a chicken farm with my husband at the time on Montserrat. This was the third attempt on the third island in as many years but this time we had the land, the resources and the support of the right government officials. But he would not take their advice. He wanted to bring in 1000 chicks to farm as broilers, the Agricultural Director said this is your first time, bring in 200. Nope, he wanted all 1000 one time.

There he was rushing around trying to get the coops ready and all the equipment in place and the chicks show up before it is all done. So, there I was with two girls and a young baby crawling around and 1000 baby chicks in my living room. Eek. They were noisy and squirmy and they kept drowning themselves while stampeding to get to the water. After three nights of that they were moved to their coops but about 100 of them were now dead. The equivalent of about US$ 1000 was gone because we did not heed advice.

More chicks and money were lost over time because the feed ran out and when it was time to butcher them there was not adequate staff to harvest them all in the shortest amount of time. This meant that for every day they were alive after the six weeks they took to mature you still had to feed them. By the end the broilers were killed but they had lost weight and you couldn't even get five dollars for one.

Learn from the mistakes and experience of others. Read continuously about your area of interest and about the strategies successful companies and individuals have used to get there. Surround yourself with people more experienced than you and take their advice. It makes no sense to repeat the mistakes of others.

FEAR FACTORS

Barriers to Financial Success

Fear Unmasked!

So much of what we do and don't do is controlled by fear. Fear is the opposite of faith, it contradicts love, and it robs you of cash. Fear camouflages itself in many different forms but the goal is the same to keep you in lack, without purpose and meaning and eventually to kill you.

The perfect love of God casts out fear (1 John 4:18). That simple reminder is worth more than the price of this book. Scholars have found that 365 times in the bible, God instructs His children not to be afraid. That is one for every day of the year. So, where do we find this perfect love and is it really all we need to eradicate fear and its paralyzing and destructive effects in our lives? My purpose here is to help you locate the areas in your life that fear has grabbed a hold and show you how God's love can overcome its power and break you free from mediocrity and poverty.

My favorite book in the bible is Joshua. It is a constant reminder to me that we don't have to give in to fear and that we can do great things regardless of what we believe are our limitations. Joshua was a man with a serious challenge. He had to pick up where Moses left off. Joshua assisted his mentor in leading the children out of Egypt, through their 40 years in the wilderness and witnessed Moses being unable to enter into the Promised Land because of an act of disobedience. Now there are over two million people expecting him to direct them into fighting battles to conquer the land that God said was theirs and he felt totally inadequate. "If Moses who walked with God and spoke to Him directly couldn't make it in, how can I, who was only an assistant and who more than likely will screw this up, do it?" he probably wondered a time or two.

Yet over and over in the first chapter of Joshua, we hear God instructing him not to be afraid. If all it took to not be afraid was hearing God say "don't fear," then most of us wouldn't be. But God does not stop there and just as He told Joshua, He says it still today "...I will not fail you, or forsake you," (Joshua 1:5). When you can recognize God's promise not to fail us then you can find the strength and the desire not to fail Him either by giving into your fears.

Fear has it uses. In certain situations it is a most powerful ally to protect your life and those of the people around you. If you trust your instincts and experience that sense of something is not right, that person does not mean me well, you will see that a healthy fear for your life will kick in and allow you to make decisions to protect yourself.

What many of us do however, is allow the feelings of fear to paralyze and keep us immobile, so we can neither save ourselves or others. There is no failure in feeling fear; the failure is in giving in to it.

Take a moment recognize it, even acknowledge that you are afraid but just as quickly remind yourself of God's word. "I don't have to be afraid because God is with me and He says if He is on my side, what can man do to me?" (Psalms 118:6).

Let us look at a few of the ways in which fear shows up to stop your dream and keep you from really reaping the benefits of a successful business.

The Fear of Inadequacy

She is a better designer than me. He is more qualified and has more money. "Your gifts will make room for you," (Proverbs 18:16).

The best example I can give of this fear is how I am feeling as I write this book. What gives me the right to think I can speak about making money, starting a business or anything else for that matter? There are a whole lot of mess ups behind me that say I may not be the best qualified to do this. What drives me on is my desire to please God rather than give in to this need to hide out somewhere and pretend I have nothing to say. It is the need to see you be better than you were yesterday because you now know that you don't have to live a life where this monster controls every thought and decision you make.

This fear of inadequacy starts for me with a thought that maybe my words are too simple and I can't write profoundly enough. Even after I conquer that battle and get to the place where I am at peace with writing a simple book that anyone can understand, the thought shifts to maybe I won't be able to finish it.

In high school my History teacher always complained to my parents that I would always start out my essays and papers wonderfully, then halfway through the process I would just get tired and jump straight to the ending. I have yet to figure out why I did that but I believe it had to do with my fear of not having enough time and the words to get it all out; or just basic impatience. For almost ten years this fear kept me from writing because I was confident that I would never be able to finish what I started. There was never enough time, enough words and certainly if I jumped ahead to how I would get it published, then for sure it was a waste of time to even write the book as there was no money to print it.

But now I have conquered that fear of completion but then more inadequacy pops up. Who will want to read it and suppose nobody likes my book? After all, I could never call myself a writer if no one bought the book.

Pull up the Roots

I am sure if we each pulled up our inadequacy tree from the roots we will find an event from childhood or some other occasion that led us to believe that we were not good enough. Mine came from a rigid religious upbringing that although we preached God's love it was heavily laced with penalties and the premise that any moral failures were terminal and unforgiveable. The truth is Jesus did not just die on the cross so we can have eternal life if we accept Him but He also died, so we wouldn't have to be condemned for our human failings (Romans 8:1).

Right now, go and look for the roots of your fear of inadequacy. Who planted it in the ground of your mind? How does it make you feel? Isn't it about time all those roots are removed? I think so. Then pull them all up.

Plant Seeds of Truth

For every excuse you can come up with to legitimize this fear, find the truth which is the opposite of what you have believed. I'll go first. I am writer. God has given me an instructed tongue (Isaiah 50:4). I have the words to express myself in a way that others can learn. Just as God promises to complete what He started in me (Philippians 1:16), I have the spirit of a finisher, I will complete this book. There is enough resources to publish this book and if all else fails, I will release it as an eBook. I will not let money or the lack of it keep me from being a published author.

Acquire the Knowledge

You also need to go beyond words and take action. In 2007 as I seriously began focusing on writing, I knew my grammatical skills were in need of work. Wouldn't you know it, but God opens the door for me to teach at the local university and end up teaching English to students who needed remedial classes. I needed that class as much as they did and so we learned together.

What ever you feel inadequate about, do the research and learn more. It is said that if you read about your area of interest every day, you would be an expert in three years. So start reading.

If you need to go back to college, take an accounting class or refine your skills in a particular area it is worth the effort to do it. Several of the entrepreneurs at YES 2006 were already actively engaged in a web design business but after attending the event, they made a decision to go off to school. From the information presented they realized not knowing other web development languages like PHP, ASP or even Flash was limiting and would be a hindrance to their company's expansion. These entrepreneurs have gone off to college and are as busy as ever, using the knowledge they gain each day in class to advance their business.

The Fear of Limited Resources

*"But my God shall supply all your need according to his riches in glory by Christ Jesus." (*Philippians 4:19)

For many Caribbeanpreneurs money is a big challenge. Especially if you have plans to open a business that requires a storefront, the high costs of rent and utilities seems out of reach. You have already gone to several banks advertising loans to help young entrepreneurs, but they have turned you down. I would call them and say "Thank you very much for denying my request." Here is why. It means any money you are about to make will stay in your hands and you won't be repaying loans or stressing about whether they are going to come repossess your mother's house because you used it as collateral.

But finances may not be your only limited resource. You are panicking because you can't find a factory to create your designs or they won't work with you because your demand is too low. Whatever the obstacle, it can be overcome. More than likely you may have to outsource that part of your business, bring in a partner or look to Asia or Latin America but it can be done.

As I mentioned earlier, not having my own computer was not going to be a limitation for me. I had a good relationship with my former employer and used their equipment until I could afford to get my own. It is really important that you stay on good terms with people. You never know when they may be in a position to help.

Use What You Have

You have no excuses for not starting your business. The time it takes you to come up with the excuse is the same amount of time you need to come up with an alternative plan. Don't believe that you need to have large sums of money to get started. Don't hold off the dream to be a filmmaker because you want to build a studio first. I know people who have spent lots of money stockpiling equipment and they have yet to write a film script. You can make movies with your mobile phone, so not owning a $10,000 camera is no reason not to start on your film dream. (Read the story of Howard and Mitzi Allen of HAMA Productions in Antigua at trulycaribbean.net.)

Being a single mother of four makes it a challenge to follow your passion and raise them as well. But I have made a commitment to let my life be the best example that their gifts will make room for them also. It calls for sacrifice but I have found that I am worth it and so are they. I am a risk taker and I have never taken any bigger risks than in the process of writing this book. I had to say no to everything that would not allow me to fulfill this passion. That included other writing projects. God gave me favor and enabled me to use my web development skills to earn money as I worked on the book. I enjoy web development because I can still work at my own pace and in my own space. There is also enough time to be with my children and to work on my writing as I am inspired.

I entrust my daily financial security to God and with His help He creates the opportunities for me to live the life I want without compromise. Giving is a big part of my life. I believe that as you continue to give you are creating a flow that must eventually return to you (Luke 6:38). It has not failed me to keep God's promises that He will restore what was lost due to fear and ignorance (Joel 2:25) and also to bless what I do according to His plan for me.

You have to let go of the concept of lack, being without daily necessities and think about the provision ahead. Even the well being of my children I give to God (Isaiah 54). There is a lot of faith and patience involved in following your passion. But anything worth having is worth working and waiting for.

Form Strategic Alliances

What I have accomplished in the past four years was not done in a vacuum and on my own. Although I have many skills, there are other people who have mastered a craft and what would take me a week, they can do in a few hours. Being in the right frame of mind and at the right space in your life will bring you into contact with those of a similar vision. Yes, you will have those who want to tag along but have nothing to add to the program but you will also meet those who are genuinely interested in helping you build your dream, simply because you share the same passion for entrepreneurship.

Bartering is still a powerful currency and one that Caribbeanpreneurs need to make use of. Don't make assumptions; discuss it with your potential business associate. The two of you need to be in agreement about the value of what you are doing and what can be traded as in kind work. I wrote features for a magazine for several issues before they were able to pay me but that was not a sore point. The magazine was a new one with limited cash and in return for my work, they used their graphics design business to help me create my promotional materials, which is essential for the work I do. I could not afford to have these things printed or designed out of my own pocket, but suddenly here was a win win situation.

When I began Victory Christian Academy, there was one employee who was necessary but I could not afford to pay. She had three children who needed to be educated and here was a chance for both of us to get what we needed. She was so grateful for the chance for her kids to receive a quality education that she worked for about four months without a salary until a local company stepped in and paid her salary and the children's tuition. You will be amazed at how blessings flow when you are open to helping others and sharing what you have. Often we are afraid to ask for assistance because we don't want anyone to know our business and in order to build relationships you must be willing to trust. Most of my strategic alliances are not with friends. We do not hang out on the weekends or spend all day chatting online. We have common goals and respect each others work and do what is necessary to help the other build their vision. The one passion we all share is a love for the Caribbean and the view that it is our time to celebrate our identity and earn an income from our sun, sea and sand and the culture that comes with it. We have found that sharing our skills helps each to be successful and in the end we celebrate when something good happens for the other because it happens for us as well.

Do you need a website? Find a designer trying to build their portfolio and have a suitable service to offer in return. Also, with so many social networks and free blogs available having a web presence is not the challenge it once was.

If you do need storefront space, you may not need to take on the commitment all by yourself. Why not look around at more established businesses and find out if they would be willing to rent you a kiosk or a few square feet to set up a table. Do you create jewelry? Find a boutique and work out an arrangement to sell your work there.

Visit trulycaribbean.net for other business start-up ideas to spark your imagination.

Fear of Failure

Before the open sign is flipped you can already see your going out of business sale and hear what people are saying.
"...I will not fail you, or forsake you," (Joshua 1:5

I know this one well but amazingly over the years it has never been able to conquer my desire to make an attempt. At the very least I am going to investigate the possibility of its success. Too often it is when I'm doing the research you meet the people who are filled with words of discouragement and advice not to try that. They are quick to share their stories of what happened when they went to the bank and who didn't bother to support their idea and on and on.

You may have people close to you who failed at something and you saw the way they were treated by family or the community and you want to avoid that at all cost. The path to success has bumps and potholes but they can be overcome. Rather than allowing other people's failures to stop you, listen to what they say and highlight the mistakes they made that led to the business closure. You don't have all the answers, so listen and learn.

In 1997, I felt the urgency to start my own business and that it was time to chart my own destiny. God had given me a vision of what was ahead and the fact that many of us were going to miss out on our life but also the return of Jesus because we were busy doing the wrong things. It was time for me to get busy doing the right things, which was simply to write and spread the word that there was more to life than this daily existence from one crisis to another, making things up as we go along. We could have a life filled with hope and peace.

What overwhelmed me was the extent of the vision I had. It seemed totally impossible with my limited abilities and resources. Furthermore, I was now regretting not taking that marketing class in college. I had more confidence in all of the things I lacked than in the ideas in my head. I certainly did not truly believe then, what I now know to be true, that God can and will do the impossible if we just allow ourselves to be led by Him. I still have not taken a marketing class but the master teacher, who is the Holy Spirit, taught me and is still teaching me what I need to know.

The failures over the years have not really been failures, as I walked away with so many lessons that help me today. The spirit of an entrepreneur never dies. It may diminish or waiver from time to time but once your eyes have been trained to see opportunities when others see distress, you find business ideas every where you turn.

The bigger the vision, the more details you need to consider and the more pieces you may need to break it into, so that you are not overwhelmed. On paper, my YES conferences have always cost hundreds of thousands of dollars but both events I have managed to do for under US$50,000 each time. I may have to forgo a fancy dinner for a house party but the results are the same, we have a great time being together. We may have to use a community center over a hotel ballroom, but with innovation and the right décor you can create positive experiences that still leave people talking.

This fear is the foundation for The Noah Principle discussed later. When you take the big picture and build it one puzzle piece at the time, you will get the outcome you desire.

Fear of Giving

"Give, and it shall be given unto you; good measure, pressed down, and shaken together, and running over, shall men give into your bosom." (Luke 6:38)

What will be left for me if I give it away? I am afraid of what people will say if they see me put a dollar or a $100 in the plate. They will say, who does he think he is? He acting like he got money, or he showing off. Only dat she have? We block our prosperity flow because we don't have the spirit of giving.

The fear of giving is a legitimate one. We are afraid that if we give to others we won't have enough for ourselves.

The story of the boy with the five loaves and two fishes comes to mind (Luke 9: 10-17). He overhears people complaining about how hungry they are and he sees the disciples motioning to Jesus that they need to send the people away. He knew that his mother had provided him with enough food for his meal and certainly it was not enough to share with more than one other person. Suppose he had considered his lunch only enough for him, then a miracle would not have taken place. Whether he offered it willingly or they came and asked, the boy said yes. When he relinquished his hold on what he had, he gave birth to a miracle that fed thousands with leftovers.

Givers cannot be Hoarders

The fear of giving and lack is not broken by hoarding but by giving. The boy placed his food in the hands of Jesus, who was concerned for everyone present. You may be feeling that no one has it worst than you but trust me if you went looking, you would find someone that does. I don't want you to give haphazardly or unconsciously. Give with a motive of blessing someone else and leaving the doors and windows wide open for God to keep his promise that He will give back to you. It is more blessed to give to someone who can never pay you back than to give to someone who you think can do you a favor later on (Acts 20:35).

Maybe you have a desire to give but what others think about you keeps your checkbook closed. Don't let what others may say or do stop your blessing flow.

One Sunday, at offering time, I opened my purse to get some money. Of course I knew there was not going to be much in there but I did think it would be more than the penny I found. Well I turned to my nephew sitting behind me and asked him if he had any offering and he said no. So I showed him my penny and he said at least you have something to give. Well the generous soul that I am offered to split it with my nephew and we had a big joke of it. He put it in the plate and we both declared that there would be more to give the following Sunday.

Next Sunday came and at offering time, he proudly showed me his dollar and I was excited to be able to give my five. I have not known a time when I released what I had in my hand no matter the size that God has not brought more. There have been times I have questioned God about the madness of it all but I can't seem to stop and I don't want to. I love being a giver. Many times my greatest giving has not been cash but ideas. There are too many great ones for me to use but always when I share with someone, I get at least three more good ones that I can implement.

I hear so many people say I want to have my own business so I can give to my church, help others in need and so on but they won't share their lunch with anyone. They won't give a single mother a hand or the time of day to people around them. You will never become a giver as a millionaire, if you are not a giver now. Money only intensifies who you are at the moment; it won't change you into something you are not. If you are selfish now, you will be more selfish as a millionaire. If you are a giver now, it will be easier for you to give as a millionaire.

Fear of Receiving

You know how to give but you must learn how to receive. For each of us to survive and be happy we need the help of others.
"For with the same measure that ye mete withal it shall be measured to you again." (Luke 6:38b)

No man is an island my Dad always tells me and that is true but as I recently learned sometimes you have to stand alone until God sends help by the right source.

There comes a point on your journey when the people and the strategies that once worked for you will cease to function as they used to. No, you haven't failed. God is now training you in a new mode of operation and the older habits and routines won't take you there. Maybe there was a season when everyone looked to you for the answers and to help them. You took pride in being a problem solver and knowing just how to pull the rabbit out of the hat to find money and come to their rescue. But ask for help? No way. Not you. Not me.

Learning to receive is an important part of being prosperous financially. On more than one occasion, I have been in this location. I was never comfortable there because I don't want to ask for help and I certainly don't want anyone to say "dem mek me up." But the road to prosperity leads through alleys where you need someone else to light your path, pay your bills, give you a place to stay and encourage you. Sometimes, it won't be your family or even your closest friends. But not to worry, God has human agents available to help you on this journey when you least expect it and even when you do. If you do not resist this process, it will be easier and before you know it you are through to the other side.

It is also a sign of your blessing, that as a giver you are open to receiving. God promises to give back to those who give to the poor and the widows and so if a time of need comes you can be sure that God will be ready to return the favor.

I have learned to say "I receive it" when someone says "God bless you" or some other positive remark. I have found it raises my consciousness and verbalizes what I want most right now which is to be prosperous in all areas. It doesn't matter that the surroundings don't look as I want them to, I am working on something of greater worth and it takes time to come into being. Learn to be gracious and thankful of every blessing you have. Receive the smile of a friend as a great gift. Accept with exuberance the kisses from your little ones. Openly acknowledge every gift, every positive word as signs of your wealth.

Fear of Equality

(Read Acts 4:32-34) What will build Caribbean wealth is not competition but unity. We each bring something worthwhile to the table to benefit all.

Look around in your community and the differences will stand out as clear as night from day. As Caribbean people we have not transferred a heritage and culture of wealth building and support to our children. We sell out our land and our companies to foreigners and the mom and pop supermarkets that we didn't feel we could run become thriving family businesses for Asians and other ethnic groups.

We go even further and choose not to support a Caribbean-owned business because we don't want them to catch up to us or exceed us. Rather than support the local store on the corner we drive miles down the road to get the same products from a foreigner. This is why we will continue to see our businesses fall apart and never expand in quality and price because we don't support each other. Money does not follow selfish and fearful people.

The move towards seeing ourselves not as a St. Martiner, Caymanian, or Montserratian but as Caribbean people is essential to overcoming this fear. We are never going to be successful if we can only see as far as our coastline. Our success as entrepreneurs is in having a regional and a global vision. This means that your success becomes my success. When I help you to open the door to your dreams, the door to mine opens as well. If we all chose to purchase clothes from our favorite local designer rather than cheap knockoffs, we would see a change in our attitudes, the way we are viewed and a renewed sense of pride in what each island can create, achieve and export.

Many dreams have died because they could not be watered in our own backyards. On many islands this attitude also permeates government and so officials are quick to place verbal and financial backing of ventures from slick talking foreigners but will not give their sons and daughters of the soil the chance to prove themselves. We have lost many of our great visionaries to other nations because we did not embrace what they saw and did not have the courage to support them regardless. Lucky for us, Caribbean people move all across the globe but never forget where they come from and they infuse this passion for the islands in all they do. It also turns into millions in remittances back home and eventually to a desire to make social and economic contributions in the region. We must be grateful but also commit ourselves to help each other out. The task of taking back our region and preserving our heritage is too big a task for one person. All of us need to be successful and we cannot accomplish this by tearing down each other or choosing to put our money elsewhere.

It is time to give our children a new legacy of teamwork and togetherness to build enterprises and nations that last.

Fear of Rejection

Nobody likes the word no. Two little letters which have broken many a heart, sank many a ship and sent many business plans into the bin.

I don't like those letters much myself in that particular combination but there is much wisdom to be learnt in hearing the word 'no.'

No sends you back to the drawing board to look for errors you missed. No allows you to break out of a tunneled vision and think outside the box or destroy the box completely. No will help build patience as you learn that anything worth having is worth fighting for.

So what do you do when the bank says no? As I said earlier, say thank you very much. But also ask them the reasons why they denied your request because it will give you clues as to what you need to improve on. Yes, I am sure you think the plan was impeccable. You even had a PowerPoint version ready for investors. There is always more to learn, so ask the questions and plug the holes in your ship.

There are instances when the plan, the collateral are all in place and you still get rejected. Don't get discouraged. There is always another way to get what you need. Sometimes it means breaking the plan down into more manageable sections. Do what ever you have to but don't give up.

The rejection you may be dealing with is not from a bank but potential clients. Keep at it. Maybe it was your approach. In the Caribbean, knowing people on a personal level is very important to doing business. "It's not who you know but who knows you," is a common refrain. In a changing work environment where so much is done electronically, it may seem quite natural to send an email and someone hires you based on what they can see on the screen. In reality, we are always more comfortable doing business with people we know.

This is not the time to be hanging with the boys at your favorite night club or beach bar. You need to get a tie on or at the very least a decent shirt. Ladies heels still work. Find out where the business professionals hang out and go have a drink. Over time, you will have the confidence to approach them and they you. It will make it easier to ask for a meeting to pitch your ideas when they have seen you in a more casual setting.

There is still a lot of chauvinism in the corporate Caribbean but do not allow that to intimidate you. Know who you are and what you want and be ready to make your sales pitch.

Fear of Success

Now what do I do with all this money? Where can I find loyal staff to help me expand?

How could there possibly be such a thing as fear of success? Yes there is. A big part of this goes back to the voices in your heard. What will people think if you start making money, if you bought your own house, stopped taking the bus?

We fear the ostracism that comes from being in a different economic bracket and people now believing that because you have money, you feel you are better than them. They will boldly tell you that or ask why the status quo is not good enough for you anymore? Mediocrity is no longer an option. Human survival requires that we overcome and excel to be able to influence others and change the world.

This fear has bombarded me a time or two. I think of what would happen if my books did sell and I had to travel to promote it. What would happen to my kids? Who could I trust to take care of them like I could? Will men no longer be interested in me because I make more money than they do or have some notoriety? The list of questions and issues goes on and on and usually you will meet people that fuel these fears.

Like every other fear you have to seek the truth that is lurking in the reflection. What if I did succeed? How could I change my life and that of my children with more money and opportunities? The answer of a future that looks like the one I desire to have for me and my little ones outweighed the fears of what could I imagined could go wrong if I was successful.

Others fear that even if they made a million today by tomorrow it would all be gone so why even try. If you take the time to acquire wealth in the right way, honestly and with the right attitude and foundation to manage it, then you don't have to be afraid of losing it. Hold it all with light fingers, not expecting it to disappear but knowing the money in your bank account is not you, it is not your true worth. For you are priceless.

There are millionaires and billionaires with no self-confidence and bad attitudes. Money won't cure a bad habit or suddenly give you self esteem. It will amplify what ever your previous attitudes were before it showed up. You may try to hide it for a while but eventually it will surface.

When you no longer fear success, failure is not a death sentence; it becomes another lesson learned that will make you more successful on your next attempt. Make adequate preparations for the changes that will come with increased business.

Will you need to hire more staff? Then begin to plan how you will attract the right employees, work out salaries and tax issues that you will have to deal with.

Will increased business mean more travel away from your family? Strategize on whether there is a friend or family member who can take care of your kids while you are away or make the investment to hire a live-in nanny.

Do not allow your business growing to catch you off guard and unprepared. Read stories of how other people worked through business expansion, encourage yourself and make a plan and by all means start expecting success.

Break Through the Barriers

All of these fears are rooted in one thing, pride. What about me? What will people say? What if this doesn't work? But what if it does? What if I can't manage the money well? Suppose I lose it all? I have nothing to start with. Use what you have in your hand.

Fear is a chameleon. We usually don't know that it is running the show until the damage is done. It disguises itself as lack, excess, anxiety, uncertainty, bulimia, overeating, depression, apathy, abuse, impatience, jealousy, selfishness, controlling and the list goes on and on. It hides under so many layers that just when you thought you uncovered them all, here comes another layer – a new issue to face.

Face your fears about your inactivity; the reason you always play it safe and never challenge yourself to be more. No longer can you use the excuse of a childhood incident or the words someone spoke over you. At this stage of your life, you must be consciously responsible and choose to live out the dreams that have been burning inside of you since you were created.

Face your fears about your spending habits. Why do I do it? What need does it satisfy in me when I spend money or horde it? Why can't I save money? When you can answer these questions...you can spend more consciously and give more consciously, always aware of the goal to be accomplished by using what you have.

There have been many people who did everything I have suggested and the bank still rejected them. Only to find out that they took your great business plan and used it to help a friend get the loan you were seeking. Suddenly your idea is now making money for someone else. You have a right to be angry but don't stay that way. This is one of the reasons Caribbean people are not open to sharing their ideas with others because they fear it will be stolen. Even with all of the copyright laws in your favor, you still must get beyond that fear and push ahead.

Your dream is your passion. Your passion is your life's work. Your life's work will cause you to prosper in all areas of life. No one can do your dream like you can. Don't worry about others that will try to copy you. They won't be able to do you. Your smile, your energy, your tenacity, your creativity, your personal touch cannot be replicated.

"For God has not given us a spirit of fear but of power and of love and of a sound mind (a mind that is clear, focused, able to see what is possible in the midst of impossibility)," (2 Timothy 1:7).

Do not be afraid to confront the things you fear. Acknowledge them and then realize that they can be overcome one thought at a time, one action at a time. Find the resources you need to alleviate the fears you may have. Make use of your local small business development office, an investment bureau, or regional resources that cater to start-ups. Take that very big dream and break it down into small manageable strategies.

Surround yourself with other entrepreneurs and also more established business persons who are willing to offer their expertise. Be willing to learn from the mistakes of others. Whatever barriers you see ahead of you, break through them and press on. The world is waiting on your gift to come to life, so get moving.

The Noah Principle

Have a Vision

My Dad pulled off a major miracle in 1999. He and his small church congregation of about 100 dedicated a three-level church facility that was built over a period of five years on nothing more than barbecues, obedient believers and generous givers. Many who gave were not members of the church or professed to be Christians but somehow he managed to spread the vision to people throughout the community and beyond. They built that church which is now valued at more than a million dollars on what I will call the Noah Principle.

God told Noah he wanted him to build an Ark. What was an Ark? Only God knew but He was going to teach Noah how to build it. Through dreams and visions, God unfolded the plan bit by bit; showing him how to design, then construct a home that was secure enough to float above the highest mountain peaks and sturdy enough to handle elephants, lions and two of every creature on the planet along with his family. (Read the story in Genesis 6, 7).

When my father told the congregation they would be building a new church, he willfully neglected to leave out monetary figures. He knew that to tell this group of mostly hotel and construction workers that over the next five years they would spend almost half a million dollars to build the edifice, would have made even the most faithful faint of heart.

Following the instructions of the Holy Spirit, he would get up on a Sunday morning and tell them that they were in need of 1000 blocks for a portion of the foundation, or 20 windows for the second floor, 100 bags of cement or whatever was needed for the coming week. Every person was challenged to give enough for 10 blocks or 100 dependent on their financial ability. By the end of the service the money for 1000 blocks had been pledged and by the next Sunday he would stand and be able to report they had been purchased and already in use. He would do this from time to time and that is how the church was built. He did not overwhelm them with the entire construction needs; he broke it down into manageable projects.

After the ribbons were cut and the invoices were tallied only God could get the glory for no one could otherwise comprehend how they had managed to accomplish such a task when their financial resources had seemed so limited.

The Noah Principle is hard for me at times, because I dream in Technicolor. My mind sees on a scale of a movie theater screen and it can be difficult to think that I won't be able to see the movie play out exactly the same way from the onset. In these moments I go back to lessons learned while pregnant. Remember the egg and the sperm that come together to make a baby. It takes nine months or 40 weeks to grow. I believe that God can make a baby in a day, just like He did at creation when He made Adam. The nine months is for the parents to transition into this new stage of life.

In the same way, it is important to start your venture on a scale that you can manage. It will allow you to adjust your thinking as your business grows. Learning how to deal with clients, how to pay bills on time, to pay yourself and not to spend all your profit the first time you get cash in your hand, are vital to long term business success.

When I created the first strategic plan for Victory Christian Academy; it included a major investment in computers, the latest technology and online virtual schools. I had even begun promoting it as such. For the school to open as I saw it, would cost more than US$ 25,000 just in technology. But as time grew closer and I realized that there was not going to be the cash to invest in the virtual school we needed another alternative curriculum fast. Amazingly I had the solution in my possession all along. In the months prior to opening, I had received catalogs from a variety of Christian curriculum providers. The one we eventually would use was affordable, quite effective but it simply did not have the bells and whistles that I wanted.

Recognizing that I was not going to turn back now, I again reviewed my options, said a prayer and selected the curriculum. ACE allowed us to order just what we needed. If we could only afford books for one week or one month for five students, that's just what we ordered and the cost was well within our budget.

The dream I thought would have to be put on hold was very much alive. In the months ahead as we began the school this principle of a little at time would serve us well. Sometimes it meant telling the staff that they would only get a portion of their salary for the moment, as we were dependent solely on tuition. I am happy to say under my management, we were never more than two weeks behind in payments. Being upfront with the staff and creating a positive working experience also meant they gave 100 percent at all times even when their salary was late because they realized we were all in it together. Always clear up any outstanding debts whether with staff or creditors. As the school continues to grow we practice this principle to manage a consistent growth and to deal with the challenges of advancing the organization.

Now having researched the virtual school more, it would not have been the right fit for our students and it would have been money wasted or a dream deferred because I was too hard headed to consider other options. Do not change your goal but strategies may have to change from time to time.

You must have a vision. What do you want to do? Why do you want to do this? How will it impact your family, your community, your world? Really check your heart to see your true motives. Are you doing business simply to make money? Even if that is so, be honest about it. Don't try to hide it behind a lot of noble clichés just to make other people happy. What ever your intentions, be clear about it, first to yourself, then on paper and then to others.

We have no knowledge that says Noah was a builder by trade and even if he had, certainly the size of the Ark was a challenge in itself. It can be quite easy to stop at the first challenge but don't. Be persistent. Take the time to see the dream in your mind. Over and over again, dream it. Visualize it. Speak it to yourself. Practice your sales pitch. See yourself on that stage performing. See the credits role on your first feature film.

If you don't have a vision for yourself, God has one waiting to share with you. Just ask and be open to receiving the answer. Some of you may be right in the middle of your destiny but can't see it. Others may be so far away that to even try to get there seems impossible. Have no fear. You still have enough time to fulfill your purpose and live the life your heart desires.

Make a Plan

Noah was given instructions on the length, height, breadth of the Ark; what it needed to be made of and for what purpose. You need to create a business plan. At the very least, I always start any new idea with a strategic plan. This is a two-page document just highlighting the main ideas, suggested company names, products and services to be offered, and a list of things that need to be accomplished before I can start.

Make a commitment. Put it in writing. This is one of the major hurdles but it will be an important marker as to how soon you will get to the end. If you are afraid to put your name and your life on the line to fulfill the dream then you don't have what it takes to carry it all the way.

Are there other people doing what you are doing in your area that will be direct competition? What will set your business apart from the other players? How will you handle distribution of your product? What will it cost to purchase the equipment you need?

Find out what it will cost you to start a sole proprietorship or an incorporated company. Even if you can only afford a sole proprietorship, go ahead. You can incorporate the company later on. Maybe you are more of a social entrepreneur. Your ideas lend themselves more towards non-profit foundations, than a corporate enterprise. Go for it. Truly Caribbean Network came out of my non-profit and was birthed from my passion to spread the gospel and using the media to do it. When I began in 1998, I had no idea that it would become the brand that it is today.

Magic Johnson is a great example of someone who has reinvented themselves; from a world class basketball champion to a successful entrepreneur. He has created a brand that works in both areas, as a major corporation and as a solid non-profit entity. There is no reason you can't have both and in fact in today's business environment, being able to show how you make contributions to your community and the wider world is a major selling tool. It is also a great way to pay your tithes. Commit to taking 10 percent of your profits, even if it is only 10 bucks at the start and donate it to a worthy cause. You will be surprised how giving increases your bottom line over time.

Seeing your ideas on paper may well be another barrier that you must break through. There is something about seeing things in black and white. Now you have to go further than the paper, you must execute the plan. Again I am always challenged here. I want all of it but I want it bad enough that I will get started with what I have available.

If you are writing a book, this is not the time to be panicking about how you will get it published. Just write. If you have a dream to start a community center with lots of great programs, don't stop because you don't know where the money will come from or how to write a grant proposal. Can you start a program using a school facility or church after hours? Look around you. Many times it is not necessary to reinvent the wheel. Join forces or use available resources in a new way.

Make the First Move

Start your business with what you already have. Victory Christian Academy was started with the last month's salary of my previous job. It meant having to alter my grand opening plans for the school but it allowed me to start on a scale that was manageable.

Do the Research, i.e. Google. There is so much information available online that with a little work, you can lay the groundwork for a successful business. I found all of the ideas for starting the school online free of charge.

If it's simply to gather the wood or clear the area where you are going to build your Ark, make the move. Your first move can include, applying for a business license and finding adequate office space or rearranging your bedroom to add a desk and chair.

For those working from home while raising a family, explain to your family and friends what you are doing and enlist their support to help you. Set proper working hours so they know not to interrupt you while you are working. This may take a bit of practice for you to separate work from home life and for them as well, so be patient but persistent.

If you are going to be baking or catering professionally then now is the time to start acquiring more equipment. You may not be able to purchase everything at the start but spend what you have to get the most important items so you can begin to earn an income.

Whatever you are doing, break it down and do not be disheartened because your start-up cash is limited or non-existent.

Consider baking one of your specialties and taking it to a major supermarket chain or special deli for them to sample. Go with a plan in your head that you want them to consider. Be proactive and suggest (put it on paper as well) that they feature your cakes every Friday in combination with one of their other treats. You know you can't handle baking 20 cakes every day to start with but you can manage five cakes for one day. Begin there.

Fashion designers, can you get a popular talk show host, news anchor, government official to wear your clothes? Be sure to get lots of photos and use them in your publicity, with their permission of course. Make it an official agreement that you sponsor the clothing for the talent and your company and brand is properly acknowledged in the credits of the show or event publication.

The goal is to become visible and to create a niche for your business. Think outside your usual box. Look at what larger companies abroad did to position them in the marketplace and find a space that you can fill in your present market.

Tell the World

Noah also had to preach during the time he was building the Ark. He warned them that a great flood was coming and if they were not ready and repentant they would be destroyed. They laughed and heckled but he pressed on because he had a word to stand on.

We tend to want to keep our mouths closed as we are afraid of what others will say and their negative responses. You will hear them sooner or later so you might as well begin. My reason for keeping quiet was often because I did not think I would live up to my word, so why share it. But often when the dream has been burning in you for so long, you will get excited and need to share it, just so you won't pop. Go ahead and do it.

Initiate contact with potential clients and begin spreading the word that you are in business.

- Launch your website or open a Facebook or other social media account and keep them updated with news about your venture
- Send out a press release to the media and blogs that target your market
- Distribute flyers
- Always have business cards on hand

Make sure that every brochure, business card, and letter you send out has a contact number and an email address where you can be reached. There are too many free email accounts available for you not to have one. The first opportunity you get to change from a hotmail or yahoo account to one from your own website, please take it. This will add to your company's image and legitimacy.

Have a list of questions that you think potential clients may want answered regarding your business. Know how you would handle shipping to an off-the-beaten track client. Be ready to rework a proposal if the first one is rejected. Be willing to adjust your strategy to reach customers.

There will be people who want to kill your dream but a God-given dream can only be destroyed by you. There is a time to keep things to yourself but eventually, like Noah your dream will become too big for you to hide. So share it boldly.

There should be no voices greater in your own ears than yours and God's. Do not allow other people's views of you, the economy or their own failures to make you lose track of the goal. Do not simply disregard them. Listen to what they say then sift through it. Throw out those things you can label as their own fears and not yours. Take the wisdom sometimes hidden in their remarks to prepare for the rough times. Say thank you and leave the rest behind.

It is important to realize that the voices which have the most power to shake you are not those of strangers on the street. It is your parents, spouse, and children, best friends, who can make you doubt your chosen profession or passion. Don't let them stop you from moving forward. There needs to be a barrier breaker that goes first and that is you.

Invest in Your Dream

No one can build this business but you. It is important that you put in the time and the money. Don't lose sight of the goal even when you must change your strategy.

This is my biggest challenge and the hardest for me to deal with. I want it the way I see it. Why couldn't I have 500 entrepreneurs at my first YES conference? It's a great idea but where are all the people? A great beginning was not impossible but when you not only have to sell the event but yourself as well, it can be a challenge to convince sponsors and other agencies to support an unproven idea.

They want to see you deliver on what you promise and that is why in many cases, it is best to start on your own before incorporating others into the vision. Caribbean people and businesses are always wary of doing business with their own and so you have a better chance of getting their financial support after you can show one or two examples of your success. This does not mean that because you have done it twice everyone is eager to through money at your venture. It will still call for hard work.

"I hate begging," is often the response I hear from people when I suggest partnering with someone else. Even for my non-profit ventures I do not like having to ask people for money. However I have learned and continue to learn how to show potential sponsors the benefits of partnering with me to build our school and our other community projects. You have to be able to show that there is something in it for them. Appeal to their desire for corporate citizenship.

Let me also add that sometimes the most important thing that a sponsor can help you with is not always cash. There are some agencies and companies that by your association with them doors are opened. Look for various ways to collaborate with non-profit or for profit companies as a way of building your business.

YES 2006 allowed me to establish great working partnerships with local and regional telecommunication companies, entrepreneurship foundations, banks and other entities who saw the benefits of promoting an event to encourage young people to start a business.

Old people say there is more than one way to skin a cat. The same is true for your business. So don't give up. Step back a bit then take another look at how you can bring it into being.

A rule of big business is never to spend your own cash but I think that is one of the major reasons many businesses fail. God began everything with a seed. He declared that as long as the earth existed, so would seed time and harvest time (Genesis 8:22). You need to invest your own time, money, energy to build and maintain your business. You actually rob yourself of the true harvest when you only use other people's cash or the banks to run your enterprise.

No Turning Back: Allowing God to Seal the Door

The Noah Principle is not for the faint of heart. It is for people who want to spend the rest of their life doing the things they are passionate about and earning a living at the same time. It gets you labels like "crazy," "fanatical," "impractical," and the list goes on. There is no other way to get a fantastic miracle, grow a company in a struggling economy, or see the impossible made possible without being ready for the name calling. As long as you can remember that the names they are calling you are just a reflection of their own fears and has no real bearing on who you are, then shake it off and move on.

We talked about shutting down the voices earlier. At every stage of the game there will be voices that you will have to shut out. Interestingly enough, some of the voices that you will have to silence coming to the end of your journey are the voices who in the early stages were cheering you on.

Many people are good at giving you their little pep talk early on. You will mistakenly believe that they really have your back and will stick with you but half the time, they are merely paying lip service. Their words were what you needed in the early stages to motivate you to go ahead with your dream and God allowed it. Now your dream is here and you are living it and they are no where to be found. What happened? They never believed that you could do it in the first place and when the name calling began they figured it best to separate themselves from you.

Surprise, surprise. You are now rolling in the dough and here they come again reminding you of that time you shared the dream with them and they encouraged you. "I knew you could do it."

"You did? So where were you when my lights were cut off? When I asked you to help me pick up my equipment and you didn't have the time?"

It would be so easy to get bitter and you would be justified because you did the work. They only had words and no action. But don't. Don't get bitter. Don't get resentful and rob yourself of the dream that you built. This is the time when forgiveness must come into play. Forgive them. They played the role they were supposed to and they went only as far as they were allowed. God has a way of doing that. He knows our need for approval; to have others who believe in us and can see what we can see but there comes a time when we must separate from all that is familiar to embrace the life we want.

Sometimes it will be family. Other times it is the job that helped you to build the business in the first place. Now you must walk away from it so you can focus on building your own dream.

Fear makes us want to hold on to the past. We want a back up plan, a just in case idea. There comes the moment when you must allow God to seal the door. When you can no longer straddle the fence and swing between both worlds. The vision is still blazing in your heart and mind and it is no longer an idea, you can see that if your just take that last step you are going to be a full-fledged entrepreneur.

Before one drop of rain fell, the door to the Ark needed to be sealed. Caribbeanpreneurs thrive best when they are in over their head. Not in debt, but you are so focused on seeing the business come to life that you know failure is no longer an option. To experience the flood you must go beyond yourself. Take a risk that challenges your comfort zone. God sealing the door means, only He can open it. You closing it, means you are at risk of drowning when the flood comes. When He seals the door you can be sure He has equipped you with the tools you need when your business takes off. Your attitude will be right, your confidence will be right and your trust will be in Him. His provision and abundance will follow.

Be Patient

Noah and his family had to get in the Ark and wait. It did not begin raining immediately. Seven days went by before it did and I am sure there were more than a few questions from his family about if he was sure he heard from God, even after 120 years of building.

People will see you putting in effort and because they see no outward fruits of success, they will question why you are doing it. Don't take them on. Stay focused. If you were filling a bucket, the water drops inside and it takes time to get to the top before it can overflow. Because you don't see any profit and your clients are few, is not a reason to give up. Work your plan. Persistence always pays off.

It is easy to forget the lessons that childhood teaches. Everything comes with much trial and error. Consider a toddler learning to walk. He tries many times before he succeeds to stand up without holding on, then later he has the courage to take a step, then another. Watching my own children through this process, it takes time and it also meant allowing them to fall at times then offering encouragement to get up and try again.

This is what I hope that I can help you do. You have fallen but you can get up again. Your first, second and third try at owning a business did not work out does not mean you are not an entrepreneur. Can you sit down and highlight why each one failed and what you did better the next time around?

When I moved to St. Kitts in 2000 to start my business, I had high hopes for its success. St. Kitts was about to take off and I was getting in on the ground floor with a venture I thought would become necessary. However, I had a dream but no capital and no real concept of how to get it off the ground. So, I took side jobs with ad agencies and production companies to write scripts for commercials and documentaries. At the same time I continued to pitch my ideas to potential clients and interviewed for jobs in my area of interest. When things got tight in my personal life the first thing I dropped was my dream. They seemed to collide and I felt I was making the best choice to try and save my marriage. It certainly seemed a convenient time to give up as the rejections seemed to be coming fast and furious and other proposals were tied up in red tape.

The first rule of doing business should be everything takes time so just learn to wait. Shortly after leaving St. Kitts, I learned two of the projects and a job offer had come through, but I was no where to be found. This action repeated itself several times in the years to come wherever we moved and I learned that it does not matter where you live, you have to wait. If you know you have planted the seeds in earnest, they will grow in the right time. Water them with your dreams, prayers, constant revising and they will come to past.

I lived on St. Eustatius in 2002, and there was a serious drought. It would not rain and so it also seemed in my business. There was no rain...Business was stagnant. By December we were moving again and wouldn't you know the rains came. A friend of mine emailed me to tell me her garden was flourishing; her pumpkins were huge and life on a whole was looking up. You just have to wait.

While you are waiting keep writing, keep designing, keep studying. Practice your craft and service the clients you have with the best you can give. Treat each person you meet as the valued customer they are. Building the discipline to manage your finances in this time when money is tight will benefit you later on. Having the right attitude during the waiting period will pay great dividends in the long run.

Strike a good balance and be sure to give yourself time to have fun as well. Don't miss the birthday parties or a chance to walk on the beach, take a hike or visit friends abroad. It won't be long before your business is flourishing and there won't be as much time for play then.

The Flood

It's here. The rains have come and clients are knocking down your door. Your inbox is flooded with requests to buy your music, invitations to perform, and interest in your work.

Now is not the time to be scratching your head, figuring out what to do. Your calendar should be open, ready to book clients. Your contracts should be available both in print and electronically for them to sign and return. Your online store is open to direct people to your site and your passport is up to date so you can travel.

When your business takes off, you must be poised to handle whatever comes and you will be. You've been praying, you've been dreaming and you have done the work to get it this far. This is not the time to get cocky but do celebrate your success. Don't run out and spend that check all in one place. Save, save, save. Save during times of plenty.

There was provision in the Ark to sustain Noah and his family for the forty days of rain and the subsequent months of waiting for the waters to recede. If you can consistently save in the times when there is more than enough...you will have something for the days when you are waiting for your next harvest or your new venture to take off.

The flood was Noah's vindication. It will be yours as well. What once seemed impossible to you, crazy and unnecessary by others will be a reality. You didn't even know the full story or why you needed to start the business. Your eyes could not see and your mind did not comprehend the full magnitude of one decision. But your vindication has come and it is raining. Congratulations.

Be careful, there is no time to gloat. God prepared you in a dark time for just this time. Get to work. The world needs you to operate your gift, your passion, your business in all its glory. When it hits you that all of your hard work has begun to pay off, take a deep breath, acknowledge the one who gave you breath and the dream and say "Thank you." Now get back to work.

I encourage you to read Genesis chapters six and seven to learn how Noah built his Ark. This monstrosity of a building came from a vision that God gave, the very measurements, materials and methodology for its construction were from his Creator. God can and will do the same for you as you work to become an entrepreneur. The times we live in, calls for dreamers and visionaries who have the strength and courage to bring dreams to life. It takes perseverance, and time and a yearning to continue to learn. Failures are not really failures if you learned something from them. Always be ready to reevaluate where your business is heading and make the adjustments to get back on the course that meets your goals.

For me the Noah Principle comes down to these mantras. Be your passion! Work your passion! Live your passion! Do you every day! Dream it! Pray about it! Speak about it! Then do it some more!

Write a Happy Ending

I have lived the concepts and principles in this book without deviation during the past year and they work. Giving up all other pursuits to sit down and write seemed pretty crazy at the time with four kids to support but I didn't feel as if there was another option. 2008 was the year I was dedicating to following my passion and write, not for other people but for me. I wrote two books, a screenplay, a pilot for a drama series, music, poetry and I began blogging intensely.

I also launched a new Truly Caribbean Woman blog which is being well received globally. On the blog you will find a new magazine for women, Truly Woman, which is the updated version of the one I let others talk me out of more than 10 years ago. Each issue is filled with inspiring stories and ideas to help women live their best life according to the principles in the Word of God.

Miracles happened when I was obedient to the Spirit and wrote as He inspired. Obstacles were great and often looked impassable but I kept my eyes on the prize even when it looked like I had lost so much by society's standards and even my family. The most amazing opportunities came my way as I got sold out to my dream. I traveled to speak at seminars and to produce life coaching episodes for the Warren Cassell Show which is aired on cable television around the Caribbean and Europe.

My words may sound as if it has been a never ending stream and flood of highs but I spent more time alone, waiting and crying and writing, then waiting some more before things began to fall into place. It is hard having the door sealed shut on you, so everything but writing seemed like a waste of time.

So how did I eat, the favor of God. Just when I needed it, an opportunity to speak or build a website would open for me to keep food in my refrigerator and a roof over my head. More than once in 2008, I had to depend on others to feed me and my children and to give us a place to live but I thank God that He had havens prepared to care for us.

Coming into 2009 was even sweeter, knowing I could show the proof of my efforts, not in dollars and cents at the start but a great sense of pride and accomplishment that my words were connecting with readers and when the flood began, I was ready. There were still fear barriers that needed to be broken and none of them disappeared by running away but by looking at them head on and standing regardless of the words being spoken, the intimidation or my own personal fears of inadequacy and insecurity about my choices.

It is raining now. Both *Guide to Good Love* and the book you are reading are going to press at the same time. All of my blogging is paying off as I now have requests for the book and events to speak at. After pitching my screenplay to several different people, things have begun to fall in place for the production of *Cayman Blues,* a feature-length romantic comedy filled with lots of my own music. How cool is that?

What I am doing would be no fun if I was the only one out here living on the edge. There are so many incredible men and women around the Caribbean and across the globe who inspire me. Whenever I had one of my "what the heck are you doing" moments, I made a call, sent an email, or surfed the web to find the latest news on other Caribbeanpreneurs.

The TrulyCaribbean.net brand is taking me places I never dreamed of; the best part is that so many people are able to take the inspiration and lessons I share and change their own lives and the world around them.

A Biblical Perspective

Whether you study the bible or not you may have heard of Noah and the Ark. I have used this story to show you that biblical principles, when applied to your God-given vision will bring forth results. What I cannot close without saying is that after the floods had receded and the world began to be replenished, God put a rainbow in the clouds. It was a promise to Noah and to all of us that never again will He destroy the world with water (Genesis 9:16). The rainbow also represents the glory of the Lord which should be present in each of us. We manifest God's glory when we accomplish the vision He sets before us.

The Ark represents a place of provision. This is your time to store up for the challenges ahead. When you follow God's instructions you will be safe in His provision and protection. The flood, yes it brought much destruction but it was also the salvation of those who believed.

There is a time ahead that will challenge the very essence of our lives. We will have to choose sides. We will have to declare whether we serve the True and Living God or man. When you follow God's instructions for your life you will do well. When you yield to the world's concept of acquiring and using wealth, destruction will be the result.

God wants to supply all of your needs. He wants wealth in the hands of those who will honor Him and use it according to His design. Will you be one of them?

If you have never accepted my Lord Jesus Christ as your Savior and Friend, I encourage you to open your heart and believe that you are a sinner in need of His forgiveness. Accept the gift of the blood of Jesus which was shed on the cross for you and confess Him as the Lord of every area of your life.

I wish you much success on your journey of faith and wholeness. God has some awesome visions in store for you to accomplish with His help. Be sure to let me know how this book has encouraged you to pursue them with all of your heart and soul.

Be blessed.

NOTES

NOTES

NOW AVAILABLE

Truly Caribbean Woman's Guide to Good Love

SEMINARS

To attend an upcoming Truly Caribbean Woman seminar or entrepreneurship event visit www.trulycaribbean.net for dates near you.

Nerissa is available to speak at conferences and to teach her *Life on Purpose and Work Your Passion* Seminars.

Contact her at:
Email: info@trulycaribbean.net
Blog: http://trulycaribbeanwoman.wordpress.com
Website: www.trulycaribbean.net

www.ingramcontent.com/pod-product-compliance
Lightning Source LLC
Chambersburg PA
CBHW071248170526
45165CB00003B/1278